LGBTQ
LiFE

When You're Ready
COMING OUT

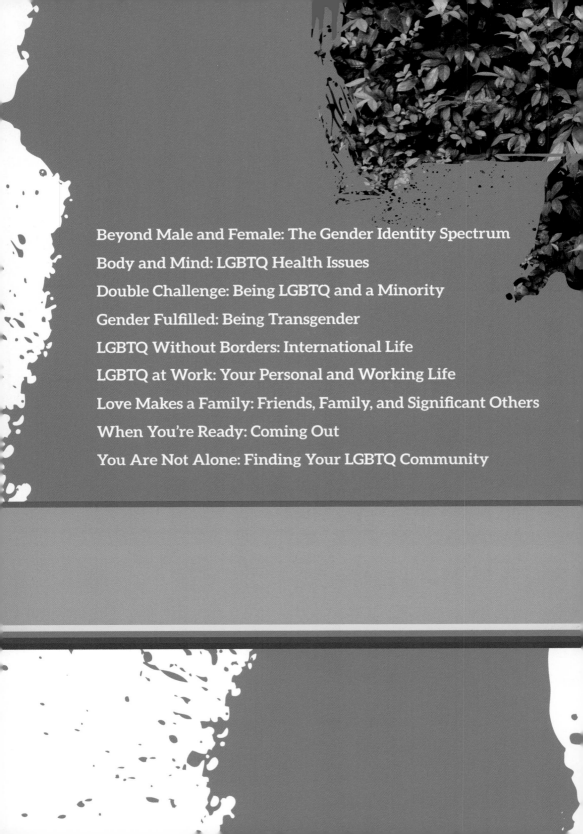

WHEN YOU'RE READY
COMING OUT

By Katherine Lacaze

Mason Crest
Philadelphia • Miami

Mason Crest
450 Parkway Drive, Suite D
Broomall, PA 19008
(866) MCP-BOOK (toll free)
www.masoncrest.com

Printed in the United States of America
First printing
9 8 7 6 5 4 3 2 1

Series ISBN: 978-1-4222-4273-5
Hardcover ISBN: 978-1-4222-4281-0
E-book ISBN: 978-1-4222-7528-3

Cataloging-in-Publication Data is available on file at the Library of Congress.

Developed and Produced by Print Matters Productions, Inc. (www.printmattersinc.com)

Cover and Interior Design by Tim Palin Creative

QR CODES AND LINKS TO THIRD-PARTY CONTENT

CONTENTS

KEY ICONS TO LOOK FOR

WORDS TO UNDERSTAND: These words, with their easy-to-understand definitions, will increase readers' understanding of the text while building vocabulary skills.

SIDEBARS: This boxed material within the main text allows readers to build knowledge, gain insights, explore possibilities, and broaden their perspectives by weaving together additional information to provide realistic and holistic perspectives.

EDUCATIONAL VIDEOS: Readers can view videos by scanning our QR codes, providing them with additional educational content to supplement the text.

TEXT-DEPENDENT QUESTIONS: These questions send the reader back to the text for more careful attention to the evidence presented there.

RESEARCH PROJECTS: Readers are pointed toward areas of further inquiry connected to each chapter. Suggestions are provided for projects that encourage deeper research and analysis.

SERIES GLOSSARY OF KEY TERMS: This back-of-the-book glossary contains terminology used throughout this series. Words found here increase the reader's ability to read and comprehend higher-level books and articles in this field.

FOREWORD

I'm so excited that you've decided to pick up this book! I can't tell you how much something like this would have meant to me when I was in high school in the early 2000s. Thinking back on that time, I can honestly say I don't recall ever reading anything positive about the LGBTQ community. And while *Will & Grace* was one of the most popular shows on television at the time, it never made me feel as though such stories could be a reality for me. That's in part why it took me nearly a decade more to finally come out in 2012 when I was 25 years old; I guess I knew so little about what it meant to be LGBTQ that I was never really able to come to terms with the fact that I was queer myself.

But times have changed so much since then. In the United States alone, marriage equality is now the law of the land; conversion therapy has been banned in more than 15 states (and counting!); all 50 states have been served by an openly LGBTQ-elected politician in some capacity at some time; and more LGBTQ artists and stories are being celebrated in music, film, and on television than ever before. And that's just the beginning! It's simply undeniable: *it gets better.*

After coming out and becoming the proud queer person I am today, I've made it my life's goal to help share information that lets others know that they're never alone. That's why I now work for the It Gets Better Project (www.itgetsbetter.org), a nonprofit with a mission to uplift, empower, and connect LGBTQ youth around the globe. The organization was founded in September 2010 when the first It Gets Better video was uploaded to YouTube. The viral online storytelling movement that quickly followed has generated over 60,000 video stories to date, one of the largest collections of LGBTQ stories the world has ever seen.

Since then, the It Gets Better Project has expanded into a global organization, working to tell stories and build communities everywhere. It does this through three core programs:

- **Media.** We continue to expand our story collection to reflect the vast diversity of the global LGBTQ community and to make it ever more accessible to LGBTQ youth everywhere. (See, itgetsbetter.org/stories.)
- **Global.** Through a growing network of affiliates, the It Gets Better Project is helping to equip communities with the knowledge, skills, and resources they need to tell their own stories. (See, itgetsbetter.org/global.)
- **Education.** It Gets Better stories have the power to inform our communities and inspire LGBTQ allies, which is why we're working to share them in as many classrooms and community spaces we can. (See, itgetsbetter.org/education.)

You can help the It Gets Better Project make a difference in the lives of LGBTQ young people everywhere. To get started, go to www.itgetsbetter.org and click "Get Involved." You can also help by sharing this book and the other incredible volumes from the LGBTQ Life series with someone you know and care about. You can also share them with a teacher or community leader, who will in turn share them with countless others. That's how movements get started.

In short, I'm so proud to play a role in helping to bring such an important collection like this to someone like you. I hope you enjoy each and every book, and please don't forget: *it gets better.*

Justin Tindall
Director, Education and
Global Programming
It Gets Better Project

Introduction

Nobody is one thing. The identities of all people are comprised of various defining characteristics and traits that are influenced by their upbringing, their heritage, their socialization, and even simply their genetics. All people should be able to take pride in those collective features that make them who they are—including their gender identity and sexual orientation.

As a teenager, coming out as lesbian, gay, bisexual, transgender, or questioning (LGBTQ) can be an experience that is at once liberating, exciting, terrifying, and complicated. Not only are you getting to know yourself better and becoming more aware of, and confident in, your sexual orientation and/or gender identity, but you are figuring out how to share that important part of your identity with the people in your life, from close loved ones and family members to classmates, friends, and coworkers.

This book certainly does not answer all the questions that young LGBTQ individuals will likely encounter as they decide they want to come out and are ready to do so. It does, however, explore a number of pertinent topics to help you feel more prepared to embrace such a significant experience, one that is ongoing as you advance throughout life.

Coming out is a personal choice for people of all sexual orientations and gender identities. Though the idea might seem a bit nerve-racking at first, the process can be liberating and empowering when done in your own time and on your own terms. Actively coming out may transpire in a number of different ways for different people, and everyone's experience will be unique. Yet, many teenagers encounter a range of similar situations along the way. So, do not think you are alone if you find yourself wondering exactly what your sexual orientation is and how it fits into the bigger picture of who you are as a human being. Or if you want to come out at school but are unsure how it might affect you academically and socially. Or if you are scared about telling your parents and want advice on when, how, and where to do so.

Within the following pages, you will discover the historical and current significance of coming out and how it can be an empowering part of existence for an LGBTQ person, as well as a bold affirmation of the community as a whole. You will learn why accepting yourself is one of the most important—and hardest—parts of the experience.

From there, the book delves into the process of coming out at home, at school, at work, on social media, or simply to the general public. Young people have many pros and cons to weigh as they select the right time to share their gender identity or sexual orientation with the people in their lives. Additionally, those people are bound to respond in a variety of ways. Some people may already have suspected you identified other than cisgender or straight. Some will be incredibly supportive and look forward to developing their relationship with you in a way that respects and incorporates this emerging information. Some may need time to understand or adjust to thinking of you in a new way. And, unfortunately, some might reject you. This book helps prepare young people for all those circumstances, while urging them to keep in mind that how other people respond is a reflection of themselves. People who respond negatively are dealing with their own insecurities, confusion, homophobia, or misunderstanding, but none of that means there is anything wrong or abnormal with your unique identity.

When it comes to school, work, and other social institutions, however, teenagers have a right to expect an environment that is safe and accepting. There are local, state, and federal laws guaranteeing a discrimination-free workplace, including Title VII of the Civil Rights Act. Schools are not as regulated, though, and while many try to create an environment that is welcoming for all students, others decidedly do not, often as a reflection of the prevalent attitudes and culture of the larger community. Teenagers can read about what to do in such situations and whom to talk to if they experience discrimination or harassment in those environments.

This book also explores the importance of making connections within the LGBTQ community and with supportive allies. It can be difficult to go through life feeling isolated or ostracized for any reason, but the good news is that you are not alone by any means. There are undoubtedly other LGBTQ youth or teachers at your school—even if you do not know them or are unaware of their identity, just as they may be of yours. In addition, there are other LGBTQ people in your community—and thousands within your state, and millions across the nation. With today's technology, you have a variety of means to connect to these people through online communities or via instant messaging and phones calls to share your similar experiences and to seek advice, encouragement, or even just a listening ear. Building up a solid support system around you—whether virtually or physically, or perhaps both—will be key to helping you feel cared about and supported if a friend or family takes the news the wrong way or if you are discriminated against at school or church. These people, your unofficial clan, will come alongside you to remind you that you are fine the way you are and that things will get better, bit by bit.

Combining a mixture of first-person stories, research from reputable agencies, and insight from national agencies that educate, support, and advocate for the LGBTQ community, this book will help you better understand what to expect as you come out, and how to navigate the process. You are who you are, and sharing that information with others gives them the opportunity to authentically love and support you as well.

Tyler Ford, an advocate for transgender and nonbinary people, was the grand marshal for the 2018 annual New York City pride parade.

1

Why Coming Out Matters

WORDS TO UNDERSTAND

CISGENDER: Used to describe someone who is not transgender or whose gender identity aligns with the one typically associated with the biological sex assigned to that person at birth.

HETERONORMATIVE: The attitude or assumption that heterosexuality is the normal and natural expression of sexuality, instead of one of many possibilities.

MARGINALIZED: Thought of or treated as if belonging to a marginal, or less important, position within a society or group.

PSYCHOSOCIAL: Relating to both psychological and social factors and how they interact.

STEREOTYPICAL: When something conforms to a common or standardized mental picture promoted by a majority of members within a group; stereotypes often represent oversimplified or prejudiced opinions and attitudes.

Coming out is an important, and often challenging, aspect of life for any person identifying as lesbian, gay, bisexual, transgender, or questioning (LGBTQ). Gender identity and sexual orientation may feel very personal and private, but they are also an important part of how we view ourselves, how we live our lives, and simply who we are.

Coming out is when people share with others that they identify as LGBTQ or a straight ally. This process can happen slowly or quickly, gradually or abruptly, privately or publicly. What is most important is that each person gets to choose personally how, when, and where they will come out to their friends, family, peers, coworkers, or other acquaintances. When individuals take control over their own coming-out experience, it becomes a wonderful tool for empowerment, advocacy, and self-fulfillment.

WHY IS COMING OUT DIFFICULT?

Even though a person's sexual orientation or gender identity is nothing to be ashamed of, many people—young and old—still feel apprehensive about the process. American culture, in general, continues to be **heteronormative**, and most people assume others are straight and **cisgender** unless told otherwise. As the Human Rights Campaign explains, people are raised from a very young age to think they should fit into a certain mold. They are informed, both directly and indirectly, that boys and girls are supposed to act in certain ways, and that it's "normal" to be attracted to people of the opposite sex.

Coming out is a deeply personal decision.

When individuals take control of their coming out, it can be an empowering and fulfilling experience.

The truth is, gender and sexuality exist on a spectrum that allows for many variations and plenty of diversity. There are asexual non-binary folks, demi-bisexual women, homosexual transgender men, cisgender straight men, and many more identities, which is why the LGBTQ community has adopted the symbol of the rainbow. The idea is that diversity makes life and social interaction infinitely more colorful and interesting. Because heteronormativity is so prevalent, however, it is common to feel confusion, uncertainty, or even doubt when you start to realize or know that you do not identify as a straight cisgender person.

The process of coming out can be challenging or intimidating for that reason, among others. Young people also may feel they are still figuring themselves out, and they worry the reaction of others will only confuse them further. Others believe that issues of gender and sexuality are intimate, and they don't feel comfortable discussing them with other people. Maybe they are nervous about bullying and discrimination, which unfortunately still occur and have found a new platform through social media.

The support of a parent or other respected adult can make all the difference when coming out.

When it comes to telling adults, such as parents, guardians, and teachers, young people may feel additional pressure or concern, because they rely on those people for their well-being, care, education, and support. If young people are rejected by the key adults in their

Coming out takes courage, but supportive friends will make the process easier.

lives, aside from treatment from peers or acquaintances, the stakes are higher. Backlash could have a more acute effect on their physical, mental, and emotional well-being.

COMING OUT IS A BIG DEAL

From a broader social and historical perspective, coming out also plays a role in advancing the visibility and equality of LGBTQ persons around the world. Through that lens, the action may be seen as a form of activism.

The idea is that homophobia and transphobia are best able to thrive in environments of ignorance and silence. Hatred is often based in fear of the unknown. When a person comes out to a loved one, they transform the LGBTQ community from being something abstract and general for that loved one to something very specific and personal. It's a lot harder for people to hold on to negative feelings toward a community once they realize they know individuals—friends, family members, or coworkers—who are part of that community.

In the United States, and globally, there is a horrible history of abuse and oppression toward people who are not heterosexual or who don't

Gender and Sex Are Not the Same

Sex and gender are not synonymous, though some people still mistakenly use the two terms interchangeably. The term *sex* refers to biological or physiological differences between male and female humans. This has to do with not just internal and external genitalia, but also the sex chromosomes and genes from which they are derived. Gender, on the other hand, refers to the broad and very complex spectrum of **psychosocial** attitudes and expectations about how the different sexes should behave and think. Whether a person is of the male or female *sex*, they often possess a mixture of feminine and masculine qualities to varying degrees that influence their *gender*. While it may sound confusing, it simply means the relationship between sex and gender is not set in stone.

conform to **stereotypical** gender norms. Non-heterosexual people were and still are prosecuted in numerous countries.

In the United States even in recent history, LGBTQ-identifying individuals could not legally get married or enjoy the same rights provided to heterosexual couples. This is partially because of statutes known as *sodomy laws*—or laws put in place that ban sexual practices outside of traditional male–female intercourse.

Talk about your sexual orientation or gender identity with a parent or trusted adult.

In the 1960s, just as the gay rights movement was taking off, several states began to enforce and sometimes rewrite these laws—which were actually meant for both straight and gay couples—to justify discrimination and suppress only non-heterosexual behavior, according the American Civil Liberties Union. Sodomy laws were used to prevent gay, lesbian, and bisexual people from raising, adopting, and having custody over their own children. They also allowed businesses to fire employees or simply deny employment to people based on their sexuality. Finally, the laws have been used by certain groups in other ways to justify violence and discrimination against the LGBTQ community.

In June of 2015, the U.S. Supreme Court ruled in a landmark decision that same-sex couples could marry. By that time, 37 states and the District of Columbia had already legalized gay marriage.

Becoming politically active can be empowering for an LGBTQ person.

But making that progress took a long time and plenty of work on the part of activists, legislators, and even just proud individuals who chose not to conform to society's standards.

I EXIST. I'M VALUABLE. AND I WILL NOT BE SILENCED.

Because of the history of discrimination against the LGBTQ community, coming out still has power and impact on both a personal and social level. Many of the themes chosen in recent years for National Coming Out Day by the Human Rights Campaign—such as "Coming Out Still

Discover the history of coming out and its public observance.

Matters" and "Talk About It"—point to the importance of the simple act of telling people you identify as LGBTQ.

Within society, there are still groups and individuals who misunderstand or dislike the idea of humans not fitting into their view of the right sexuality and gender. More often than not, they are scared of anything or anyone being "different." In order to maintain their preferred social order, these groups try to keep members of the LGBTQ community **marginalized**, or invisible. Although resisting being marginalized or even just openly existing as LGBTQ can take immense courage, it is vital that members of community and their allies continue to do so. That is why coming out is often still considered a form of activism.

Coming out is a way to say, "I'm here. I exist. I'm valuable. And I will not be silenced." When popular or powerful members of society come out publicly, they are raising awareness of, and giving a voice to, the LGBTQ community. They are helping to debunk the idea that any sexuality or gender identity is more normal or more important than the others.

NATIONAL COMING OUT DAY

To promote awareness of the LGBTQ population, National Coming Out Day is observed each year on October 11—and October 12 in some parts of the world. The day was first observed in 1988 in the United States and has spread around the world since then. The founders, political leader and activist Jean O'Leary and psychologist Robert Eichberg, selected October 11 as National Coming Out Day because it is the anniversary of the 1987 National March on Washington for Lesbian and Gay Rights. In an interview in 1993, Eichberg said, "Most people think they don't know anyone gay or lesbian, and in fact everybody does. It is imperative that we come out and let people know who we are and disabuse them of their fears and stereotypes."

Coming out is a way to say, "I'm here. I exist. I'm valuable. And I will not be silenced."

By living openly and proudly embracing their identity, LGBTQ young people are also giving an important voice to their community and acting as their own advocates.

MAKING IT PERSONAL

That's all fine and well for celebrities or high-ranking politicians to come out, you might be thinking. *After all, those people have the benefit of status and money to help protect them against backlash. But what about me?*

Professional athletes, celebrated performing artists, and other public figures have a broad platform for making a difference when they come out. But don't discount the impact you can have, especially

within your own social spheres. By living openly and proudly embracing their identity as lesbian, gay, bisexual, transgender, non-binary, or genderqueer, young people are also giving an important voice to their community and acting as their own advocates. They bring awareness to the people they know at school, places of religious worship, work, and home. Who knows what the trickle-down effects of that action could be? Maybe it will cause a friend who struggles with homophobia to re-evaluate their prejudice, or maybe it will give courage or a sense of camaraderie to a fellow student who previously felt scared and alone.

Coming out is a way of continuing the process of being true to oneself.

Perhaps most importantly, coming out is a way of continuing the process of being true to oneself. Even though a person's gender identity and/or sexual orientation is just part of who they are, it is an important part of how they perceive themselves, whom they are attracted to, whom they love romantically, whom they partner with, and much more.

Once you are confident and comfortable with yourself and your identity, you get to share that with other people, especially those who are close to you. By telling others how you identify, you give them the opportunity to love you as you truly are, without any false assumptions or ignorant expectations.

Even though a person's gender identity and/or sexual orientation is just part of who they are, it is an important part.

TEXT-DEPENDENT QUESTIONS

1. Why are some people still nervous or scared to come out as LGBTQ?

2. What is the relationship between sex and gender?

3. Why was October 11 chosen as National Coming Out Day?

4. How can coming out be a form of activism?

RESEARCH PROJECTS

1. Research a celebrity or public figure of any kind, past or present, who identified as LGBTQ, and write down why you admire that person. Think about whether you feel comforted or empowered knowing a person you look up to is also on the LGBTQ spectrum.

2. Investigate to see what sodomy laws existed in your state in the past, or which ones still are on the books today. Figure out how they could be used to limit the rights of people who identify as LGBTQ.

3. Talk to an adult you know who is publicly out. Ask them about their coming-out process and why they thought it was important to do it in the way that they did. Was the experience empowering?

4. Think about ways you can participate in National Coming Out Day, as either a member of the LGBTQ community or an ally. What can you do to demonstrate your own pride or support others?

2

Meet ... Yourself

CISNORMATIVE: *The general assumption that the norm is for people to identify with the gender typically associated with the sex they were assigned at birth.*

CONDITIONING: *The process of being influenced to hold certain beliefs or perspectives that humans undergo as part of growing up and learning about the world in a particular environment.*

GENDER EXPRESSION: *How you present yourself or communicate your identity, from masculine to feminine, and everything in between, to others through external means.*

GENDER IDENTITY: *A person's inherent sense of self in terms of being female, male, neither, or some of each.*

In the opinion of 15-year-old Tori Rinard, who identifies as bisexual and female, "When you're coming out, the hardest part is saying it to yourself."

That was the most difficult step in the process for her, "because [that identity] is so different from what everyone around me was," she says.

No matter how open-minded and accepting of diversity a person might be, it can be difficult to acknowledge that their identity diverges from the heteronormative and **cisnormative** expectations embedded in society and still heavily reinforced by many cultural and social entities. The first step in coming out is to get to know yourself, which takes honesty, self-awareness, and courage.

OPENING UP YOUR MIND

Different people will become aware of their sexual orientation and gender identity in various ways. No two stories are exactly the same, but it can be common to feel an array of emotions—relief,

Often, the hardest part about coming out is being able to say it to yourself.

pride, uncertainty, vulnerability, confusion, fear, affirmation, and/or empowerment. It is perfectly okay to experience any or all of these feelings at some point. It simply means you are opening yourself to the idea that you are embarking on your own human experience, and that is truly when coming out begins.

People's ability to identify and accept who they are can vary, depending on their environment, **conditioning**, socialization, education, and other factors. Someone who comes from a very open-minded, accepting home or who has strong LGBTQ role models already in place in their life may have an easier time coming to terms with their identity than a person raised in a restrictive household where any identity besides cisgender and heterosexual is demonized.

Figuring out one's own identity is an ongoing process, but try to think of it as a meaningful one. You are getting to know yourself and discovering your place in the world.

It can be common to feel an array of emotions when you become aware of your sexual orientation or gender identity.

SILENCING THE NEGATIVE VOICES

Even for Tori, acknowledging that she was bisexual meant confronting and disowning negative, inaccurate stereotypes she had heard, such as that bisexual humans are simply greedy, going through a phase, or just can't make up their minds. When she came out to her mom in middle school, she knew instinctively that her mom's reaction would be positive. Even still, she had to dismiss what she had often seen portrayed in movies or television shows, where children are ostracized by their parents or kicked out of their homes after coming out.

Figuring out your own identity is an important and meaningful process.

It took support and even prompting from her mother for Tori to then address her sexual orientation with her father a few months later, but she was starting to feel the pressure of not being able to face a person she loved and trusted and state, "This is who I am." Tori remembers when she and her father finally talked about her identity in a Wal-Mart parking lot, she cried several times, but it was a calming conversation, because all her worries and anxiety "kind of melted away."

The benefit of being honest with her birth parents, as well as her stepfather, was knowing their support and love for her were genuine. The message she kept in mind was that even if she were to lose a relationship with a given person, she would be gaining a community that would stand beside and support her.

No one can assign you an identity.

"There will always be people out there who will love and accept you, even if it is not who you expect," she says.

EVOLVING GENDER AND SEXUAL IDENTITIES

In recent years, there has been an influx of recognized terms for sexual identities beyond lesbian, gay, bisexual, and transgender, some of which may overlap. There are numerous people who identify as agender, gender fluid, metrosexual, third gender, gender-nonconforming, genderqueer, and bigender, as well as those who also might identify as aromantic, asexual, bicurious, demiromantic, demisexual, or pansexual—and this list is neither exhaustive nor inviolable.

Some people feel comforted and legitimized to have a precise label or category with which they can associate their gender identity and sexual orientation, while others may find labels to be limiting or overly simplistic. They don't want to tie themselves to a single term, or even a couple.

As the Trevor Project emphasizes, no matter how a person walks, talks, dresses, acts, loves, or otherwise lives their life, no one can assign them an identity or choose how to label them—not even parents, siblings, teachers, or other authority figures and loved ones.

You should feel empowered to personally choose the terms and pronouns you wish to use to describe yourself. Also, be aware and respectful of what labels other people may choose for themselves.

 Young people talk about embracing their identities, finding support, and coming out.

Bisexual Versus Pansexual

The term *pansexual* is just one of several terms that went into more widespread use during the first decade of the 21st century, although the concept dates back a couple of centuries at least. Pansexuality can sometimes be confused with bisexuality, but the two sexual orientations have distinctions. Bisexuality means being capable of feeling sexual, emotional, or romantic attraction to more than one gender or sex. Being pansexual, also occasionally referred to as *gender-blind*, means a person can feel sexual or romantic attraction to any other human, regardless of their biological sex, gender identity, or gender expression. In that sense, pansexuality is broader in scope.

Be respectful of what pronouns other people go by.

Several terms covering a range of sexual orientations and gender identities have come into more widespread use in the 21st century.

Orientation, identity, and tastes may change as you grow and mature.

Get into the habit of asking others what gender pronouns they go by, or how they like to be referred to. As best you can, do not misidentify another person. When in doubt, use gender-neutral terms.

WHAT IF I CHANGE?

Humans are constantly evolving in many ways. Sexual orientation and gender identity are a just couple of areas that might fluctuate as well. Even as a teenager, Tori knows that her tastes and preferences may change as she continues growing and maturing.

"No matter how old or how young you are, you're always going to be learning new things about yourself," she says.

She acknowledges that she may eventually discover that she swings more toward men or that she doesn't feel sexual attraction to them at all and could choose instead to identify as a lesbian. Her fear is of people responding that she lied before or that her past relationships were not genuine. However, that is decidedly not true.

Some people have embraced the word queer as an act of defiance.

In the same way people are continually exploring their preferences and proclivities in other areas of life, they may discover new facets of their gender identity and/or sexual orientation later. Simply because they have come out to others, or have shared preferred pronouns or a certain identity, does not mean they have to (or will) identify that way forever. Sexual orientation, **gender identity**, and **gender expression** all exist as continuums along which a person might move or vary over the years, months, or even weeks.

This idea that nothing is set in stone may sound a little frightening, but it can also be very exciting and liberating. You are free to discover

It is not uncommon for adolescents to experience same-sex attraction.

Exploration is part of pursuing fulfilling relationships.

IDENTIFYING AS QUEER

The term *queer* as a gender identifier has a controversial origin and evolution. Some people find the word incredibly offensive, because in the past, it has intentionally been used in a pejorative manner to dehumanize and degrade non-cisgender, non-straight individuals. Others have embraced the term queer, or reclaimed it, as an act of defiance. They also find value in how the term can be inclusive of the entire community or appropriate for describing fluid identities, according to PFLAG. Because the term is controversial, though, it should *only* be used to self-identify or when another person has specifically self-identified as queer.

new parts of yourself as an individual and the best ways to be fulfilled and content as you live your life.

EMBRACING NEW EXPERIENCES

As a person finds ways to have new, enlightening experiences in a safe environment, they need to be honest with themselves about what makes them comfortable, what makes them uncomfortable, and the pace at which they choose to experiment or explore. As young people become more aware of their emerging sexual, emotional, and romantic attraction during middle and high school, it is normal to want to explore this attraction and the feelings that go along with it. That's part of coming to terms with who you are and pursuing fulfilling relationships.

It is important to protect yourself physically and emotionally.

It is not uncommon for adolescents to experience same-sex attraction in addition to opposite-sex attraction. Because LGBTQ youth often begin questioning and becoming more aware of who they are during their middle and high school years, they may be sorting through all types of emotions and figuring out what they mean. This often occurs as part of interacting with their peers in a wide variety of relationships.

PROTECTING THE BODY, HEART, AND MIND

Regardless of a teen's sexual orientation and/or gender identity, it is important to protect oneself not only physically, but also emotionally and psychologically. In terms of physical precautions, teenagers can reduce the risk of contracting (or spreading) a sexually transmitted infection (STI) by always using protection, getting tested during a medical exam, knowing each sexual partner's history, limiting the number of sexual partners, and getting vaccinated.

Just as importantly, young people should also be guarding their emotions and minds—and this is true no matter how one identifies. Just because a person identifies as gay or lesbian does not mean they have to be attracted to *all* boys or girls, in the same way heterosexual individuals do not necessarily experience attraction for all members of the opposite sex.

Sometimes you need time to process your emotions after a sexual experience.

Do not let anyone pressure you into trying something physical before you are ready. If you do try something new with a sexual partner, and it makes you feel uncomfortable or confused, you do not need to engage in the activity again with that person, or with anyone else in the future, for that matter. Sometimes people need time to process their emotions and thoughts after a sexual or intimate experience to see how it truly makes them feel. You have the right to change your mind, to say no to someone you previously said yes to, and to take your time exploring the physical side of a relationship even with someone you love and trust. Your comfort zone may also vary simply based on the person you are sharing a relationship with.

TEXT-DEPENDENT QUESTIONS

1. What are common emotions a person might feel while becoming aware they are not heterosexual and/or cisgender?

2. Why might some people find labels reassuring, and other people find them restrictive?

3. What are ways that a person can protect themselves emotionally and psychologically, as well as physically, while having new experiences, intimate or otherwise, with various romantic or sexual partners?

RESEARCH PROJECTS

1. Research the financial costs associated with physically transitioning. Do insurance companies generally pay for procedures such as hormone therapy or gender confirmation (also known as *sex reassignment*) surgery?

2. Look up glossaries of LGBTQ terms from organizations such as the Human Rights Campaign, the Trevor Project, and others. Are there any terms that seem familiar or generally describe how you feel about yourself? What do you think about adopting or embracing these terms?

3

Coming Out to Family and Friends

WORDS TO UNDERSTAND

ALLY: *A term for any person who does not personally identify as LGBTQ but who shows support and advocates for the LGBTQ community and individuals.*

FAITH COMMUNITY: *A social group with members who share a particular set of religious beliefs to which they are committed in varying degrees.*

PREFERRED GENDER PRONOUNS: *Third-person words used to substitute for an individual's name (including her, she, him, he, they), which are chosen by individuals themselves to better reflect their identity.*

RELATIONAL SUBGROUPS: *Groups of people that form around a sense of overlapping identity or because of a specific social affiliation.*

When the time is right, you will feel ready to share your gender identity or sexual orientation with another person. Especially for the first conversation, people tend to select a person they have a reason to believe they can trust to love and support them unconditionally, someone they know will be a reliable **ally**. For some, this may be a parent or their siblings; for others, a friend or peer. The confidant may already have an idea about how you identify in terms of sexual orientation or your **preferred gender pronouns (PGPs)** based on previous conversations or events.

Other young people find it easier to first talk to an adult with whom they do not share an especially crucial relationship, such as a school counselor, teacher, or therapist. Because that person is an objective third party, it may feel like there is less risk involved by disclosing such intimate information, and that helps ease the fear of rejection.

There is no right or wrong path as you come out. You have the power to choose whichever one makes you feel comfortable and empowered by the process.

You may find it easier to first talk to an objective third party.

WHEN YOU ARE READY

When coming out to a friend, family member, or other acquaintance, there are plenty of ways to do so, such as in-person conversations, e-mails, telephone calls, and text messages. Even if a person lives far away, their support and encouragement can go a long way in helping a teenager who identifies as LGBTQ feel more confident and secure in their identity.

According to the Trevor Project's resource guide, "Coming Out As You," it can be helpful to prepare oneself for having coming-out

If you are ready to come out to someone, consider how they might respond.

conversations, and there are plenty of ways to do that. For example, before coming out to a particular person, the guide suggests testing the waters by bringing up a topic related to LGBTQ issues, people, or politics, including a current or historical event, or maybe an interesting subject you read in a book. Ask for their thoughts and opinions. Depending on how they respond to the subject, as well as the terms they use when referring to LGBTQ individuals, you can more effectively gauge how they might respond to you personally coming out.

Other questions to consider when determining if you are ready to come out to someone include the following:

- How does that person react when they are angry or upset with me? Do I still feel safe and loved?
- Is that person's **faith community** accepting of LGBTQ individuals and lifestyles, or does it generally denounce any gender identity or sexual orientation besides cisgender and heterosexual?
- Do they watch movies, read books, or consume other entertainment and information featuring LGBTQ relationships or characters?

Although the answers to these questions do not definitively predict a person's reaction, they might help a young person weigh whether it is the right time to come out to them, or how they could potentially react.

FINDING THE RIGHT RESOURCES

If a teenager already has an adult or peer who is supportive of them, they can use that person to practice a conversation with someone else who might not receive the news as well. Under many circumstances, positive or negative, the person on the other end of the conversation may have questions as they come to terms with the new information—just as teens may have questions themselves as they make discoveries about their own gender orientation and/or sexual orientation. Going into those complex conversations armed with information and civility can help you feel more empowered and confident to answer questions and articulate your thoughts when coming out.

LOVE IS A FAMILY VALUE

PFLAG CANADA

WE L
OU
GAY S

PFLAG CANADA

PFLAG CANADA

YOU ALWA HA

Contact PFLAG to speak with a parent of another LGBTQ person.

Young people seeking an adult to give them guidance or insight can contact their local PFLAG chapter—to name one organization—and speak with the parent of another LGBTQ individual to get insight about how their own parents might respond to their coming out. Many organization, such as the Human Rights Campaign, also have informational booklets or other documents that young people can share with parents, guardians, family members, or friends to give them helpful information and insight into the LGBTQ community.

There is no right or wrong time or location for coming out.

SELECTING THE BEST TIME AND PLACE

Some individuals may choose to come out selectively, telling specific people at a specific time and in a specific place. Others may choose to come out in one social sphere or group, and not in others.

There is no right or wrong time or location for coming out to a friend or family member. The appropriate environment for that conversation may change based on logistics (for instance, if the loved one lives in a different state) or personal preferences. In the process of selecting when to have a conversation with someone, whether it is in-person or over the phone, consider whether there might be external circumstances causing stress at the moment—such as a time-consuming school assignment, a deadline at work, or a holiday season.

Another consideration to make is whether there will be adequate time for both parties to say what they need or wish to say. If a person is feeling relaxed, focused, and willing to listen, they may be more receptive to the news and have a more desirable reaction.

Likewise, choosing an appropriate location for the conversation can also be important. When selecting the place to have the conversation, a young person might want to consider whether they feel safer talking in public or private, whether both parties will feel comfortable in the selected location, and whether to choose a spot with particular relevance to both individuals. When selecting an environment, try to make it conducive to having an important and intimate conversation with someone who means a lot to you. That can help you both feel more safe, comfortable, and willing to open up.

Choose a location for the conversation where both of you will feel comfortable.

Learn more about coming out and how you have the right to choose when and where to share your identity with other people.

Not everyone has the opportunity to come out the way they want.

"IF I COULD"

Kristain Harvey, a 28-year-old woman from Montana, did not have the opportunity to conduct the experience of coming out to her parents as she would have wanted.

Emerging into young adulthood, Kristain began seeing—or in her words, being "more than friends"— with Cin, who identified as a woman at the time and has since come out as transgender. Because Kristain knew that her family would not be very supportive of them sharing a romantic relationship, they initially kept their interactions secretive, even platonic. For a long time, because of her upbringing in a devoutly religious home, Kristain suppressed her feelings, simply telling herself that a relationship was not possible, that "it can't be a thing."

At the time, Kristain worked with her current partner at a retail store. One Sunday morning in the month of May, she remembers, the two had a conversation where Cin asked Kristain, "If you could, and I asked you, would you go out with me?" Kristain recalls answering, "Yeah, I definitely would if I could."

Soon after she gave that answer, Kristain decided that while she had convinced herself she simply *couldn't*, the truth was that she *could*. She *could* acknowledge she was romantically and sexually attracted to this person, regardless of their gender.

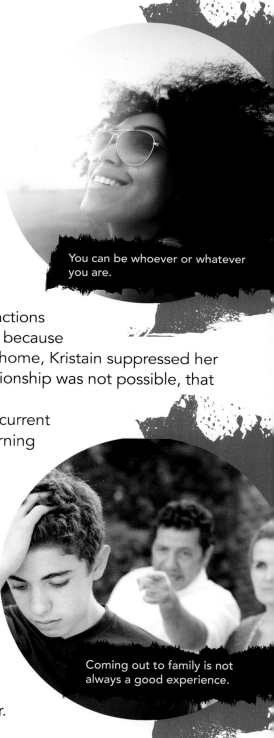

You can be whoever or whatever you are.

Coming out to family is not always a good experience.

She *could* have the relationship she desired. She *could* be whoever or whatever she was.

"I found my person," she says.

That did not make it easier, however, when Kristain's mother found Kristain's phone and saw text messages shared between Kristain and her partner that revealed the nature of their relationship. When Kristain's mother confronted her about the text messages, she made it clear she believed Kristain was doing something wrong that would negatively affect her life. Because family is incredibly important to Kristain, her mother's initial response was hurtful. And when she and her partner announced their engagement and sent a photograph to other family members a few years later, it was likewise poorly received.

"Family-wise, it was never a good experience," Kristain admits, adding that relationships had slightly improved over time but were still a bit strained.

You have the right to express your true identity how you wish.

Transitioning the Physical Self

During the coming-out process, some people who identify as transgender (or other diverse identities, such as genderqueer, bigender, gender non-conforming, or another gender) choose to transition physically, as well as transitioning in other ways, such as socially or legally. Others choose not to because of cost, medical conditions, or other personal reasons. The physical steps a person might elect to take could include hormone replacement therapy, alterations to physical appearance, or gender confirmation surgery. Just because a person decides not to transition physically at a particular time, however, does not mean they cannot rightfully identify themselves as transgender. Only you can fully know your true identity, and you have the right to express it how you wish when the time is right for you.

FACING YOUR FAMILY

It can be difficult when family members respond negatively, as Kristain's did. "You definitely have to learn to be okay with people not being okay with you," she says.

Depending on how a person was raised, they may be expecting an unaccepting reaction. For others, the disapproval may come as a surprise. Regardless, facing that kind of reception to news about one's gender identity or orientation can acutely disheartening and painful. After all, family is a highly valued **relational subgroup** with deep roots, and we expect our family to be there for us in ways other humans are not.

Young people who are worried about their parents, guardians, or other family members being especially unsupportive may want to have a back-up plan for housing, food, transportation, finances, and other essentials. While many young people may grow closer to

Facing a negative reception to coming out can be painful.

You may want to have a backup plan for housing and other essentials.

their family by being honest, the unfortunate reality is that situations arise in which parents or guardians are physically and/or emotionally abusive, or teenagers are forced to leave their home. In weighing the pros and cons of coming out to parents, if you worry about your well-being, you can choose to wait until you have already left home or until you have devised a contingency plan for where you can go if necessary.

"I AM WHO I AM"

Although Kristain knew that her family would not be accepting of her identifying as not straight, hiding who she was caused even more internal conflict and made her feel uncomfortable with her identity. She knew that it would be more damaging to her emotionally and mentally in the long-run than dealing with strained familial relationships.

"Hating yourself is not good," she says. For young people weighed down by fear about how their family will respond, or living in an oppressive environment, she adds, "Remember, you can get out of it. It may not be easy, and it may not be right away, and you may constantly struggle—just hold on," she says. "You can find family in your friends and the people you're with."

What Kristain found was freedom in saying, "I am who I am, and I'll find people who are okay with it."

You can find a sense of family and belonging in your friends and the people you're with.

TEXT-DEPENDENT QUESTIONS

1. Is there a right or wrong way of coming out to family members, friends, and other loved ones?

2. What are a few ways to gauge a person's attitudes or beliefs about the LGBTQ community?

3. How does the history of the term *queer* influence the appropriateness of its use as a gender identifier?

RESEARCH PROJECTS

1. Write down your greatest fears about coming out, to a specific person or in general. Next, think about your response to each fear or risk, and what you have to do in the face of each one.

2. Look up information packets, brochures, or other resources you could share with friends, family members, or other loved ones to answer their questions or better help them understand where you are coming from.

4

Coming Out at School, Work, and More

HOMOPHOBIA: A fear or aversion to gay and lesbian individuals that can lead to prejudice and other negative behaviors. This term is more widely used than biphobia—an aversion to bisexuality and bisexual people—and transphobia—an aversion to transgender people—but they are all related adjectives that denote anti-LGBTQ bias.

IDENTITY DISCLOSURE: Closely related to coming out, but broader in scope, this relates to the act of revealing any secret or private aspect of your identity to other people.

OUTING: Publicly declaring or spreading information, whether intentionally or accidentally, about a person's gender identity or sexual orientation without their consent.

After or while coming out selectively to individual people or small groups of friends and family members, young people must also weigh the pros and cons of coming out in broader social environments, such as school and work or within volunteer groups, religious organizations, and clubs.

There are a number of things to consider, and strategies to employ, as you work to manage your **identity disclosure** in a number of relational or social contexts. The goal is that your coming out, which has important implications for your well-being, is able to be conducted in a way that makes you feel safe, assured, and supported.

COMING OUT AT SCHOOL

Middle and high school students spend a substantial amount of time on school grounds, before, during, and after classes and extracurricular activities. Coming out in this social realm is an important decision.

Before coming out at school, students should be aware of the policies and laws in their area. For instance, transgender or gender-expansive students may experience challenges if they attend a

Some school districts are overtly inclusive of all orientations.

single-sex/gender school, and LGBTQ students might not have their identity readily accepted at certain conservative religious schools, according to the Gay, Lesbian, & Straight Education Network (GLSEN). Some school districts are overtly inclusive of students of all gender identities and sexual orientations, and may even provide them with support services and programs, or for transgender and non-binary students, locker rooms, bathrooms, and other things to meet their needs. Other schools prohibit same-sex partners from purchasing "couple" tickets to a school dance or discipline homosexual behavior. It varies based on the location of the school district or the school's unique climate and culture.

GLSEN suggests that students first talk to a trusted teacher, counselor, or other educator at their school to find out what protections

School GSA clubs provide a safe place for LGBTQ students.

Not everyone will assume or respect that your identity is confidential.

are in place for students who identify as LGBTQ. That adult figure then may be able to assist the student in approaching administration at the school to further explore which support services are provided.

CONTROLLING WHAT IS SHARED

As a student decides to come out to various peers, teachers, coaches, or others at school, they should also inform those people of whether the information is public and whether they would like the news to get

JOINING A GSA CLUB

Many middle and high schools have GSA clubs, which are student-run organizations that provide a safe place for LGBTQ-identifying students to meet, support one another, and discuss issues related to gender identity and expression and sexual orientation. The GSA Network was originally established in the 1980s, with the acronym formerly standing for Gay–Straight Alliance. The three functions of GSA clubs are support, socialization, and networking, and these groups can connect students to statewide and national campaigns on a variety of LGBTQ issues. You can find out whether your school has a GSA club, or if not, maybe you will decide to establish one yourself to give other LGBTQ students a safe place to socialize and connect.

around. Not everyone will automatically assume or respect that the information is confidential.

Some students find it easier to share their sexual orientation and/or gender identity and expression with only a couple people, but they are unconcerned about the information spreading. Others prefer to conduct and monitor their coming out experience at school and among classmates carefully.

Being very clear with each individual about your wishes is important. Otherwise, there is a risk of them **outing** you accidentally or negligently because they believe your identity to be common knowledge.

LGBTQ high school students share their experiences with GLSEN and talk about the impact of GSAs and the Day of Silence.

RESPONDING TO HARASSMENT

Unfortunately, **homophobia**, or other anti-LGBTQ bias, still exists and can manifest itself through bullying or harassment of various kinds—physical, verbal, or on social media. Sometimes this negative and damaging behavior is perpetuated not only by classmates, but also teachers, staff members, coaches, or other school employees.

As PFLAG points out, all students have the right to a safe and affirming learning environment. If a student is experiencing harassment from a peer or school employee, they should report the incident to a member of the administration. Of course, this can be a difficult or stressful thing to do, particularly if you do not know your school's discrimination or bullying policies. Students who are nervous about talking to an administrator alone can first speak with a supportive teacher, mentor, or other adult. There is someone on campus who will provide support—you just need to find them.

Homophobia can include bullying on social media.

If you're experiencing harassment, report the incident to your school's administration.

Many schools are required by law to respond to reports of harassment and bullying. School administrators should deal with an LGBTQ student's situation and provide anti-bullying solutions. If they do not, the student should express their concern to a parent or other authority figure. They also can contact a local chapter of PFLAG, the American Civil Liberties Union (ACLU), or another organization or agency with the resources to provide intervention and support.

COMING OUT AT WORK

Older students with jobs may also consider coming out at their place of employment, which has a similar set of pros and cons.

Legally, Title VII of the Civil Rights Act of 1964 forbids any employment discrimination based on gender identity of sexual orientation, protections that are interpreted and enforced by the Equal Employment Opportunity Commission (EEOC), and therefore apply regardless of contrary local or state laws. According to the

Depending on the views of your co-workers, coming out at work may be risky.

EEOC, LGBT-related claims that would be viewed as unlawful sex discrimination include failing to hire someone specifically because they are transgender; not offering an employee a rightful promotion because of their sexual orientation or gender identity; firing an employee who is planning to make, or has made, a gender transition; or harassing an employee because of their sexual orientation or gender identity.

Even still, depending on the environment cultivated at a teenager's place of employment, or the views and behaviors of managers and/ or coworkers, coming out may seem risky. It's a good idea to closely review any employee handbook or other information given to learn about the business' specific policies and procedures regarding workplace harassment or anti-LGBTQ discrimination. You can also talk to a human resources representative to confirm that you will be treated fairly and to start building a connection in case you need to report an incident later on.

It is unlawful to discriminate against employees based on sex stereotypes.

Social media is an important terrain for LGBTQ youth to navigate.

TITLE VII PROTECTIONS

The text of Title VII of the Civil Rights Act is fairly basic, prohibiting discrimination against employees based on sex, race, color, national origin, and religion. It has taken several United States Supreme Court and lower court decisions since 1964 to clarify which anti-LGBTQ practices count as sex discrimination under Title VII. For instance, in the 1989 case of *Price Waterhouse v. Hopkins*, the Supreme Court ruled that it is unlawful to discriminate against employees based on sex stereotypes, or assumptions about how people of a certain sex or gender should dress or act. This decision set a precedent for several other federal court cases that helped define what is considered unlawful discrimination based on a person's sexual orientation or gender identity.

TAKING IT SOCIAL

Social media are an increasingly prevalent part of people's lives. Facebook and Instagram are two of the largest social media hubs, but new online communities are always popping up, especially those that serve a niche demographic or are focused on a shared interest. Social media change the landscape within which young people negotiate their lives and present challenges in managing one's public and private identity, according to a 2018 study published in the *International Journal of Environmental Research and Public Health*. For LGBTQ youth, this is one more terrain they must navigate in terms of coming out.

A 2013 study by GLSEN, titled "Outline Online," which surveyed more than 5,600 students, found that LGBTQ teenagers experience

LGBTQ teens experience nearly three times as much bullying online as non-LGBTQ youth.

Revealing your identity on social media can provide access to social support.

nearly three times as much bullying and harassment online as non-LGBTQ youth. LGBTQ youth also were twice as likely to have been bullied via text message. This experience can severely damage a student's self-esteem and lead to higher levels of depression and even to poorer academic performance.

WHAT CAN HAPPEN ONLINE?

Identity disclosure on social media sites where teenagers use their real names is hard to manage, and selective disclosure is nearly impossible. The information you present on your social media profiles—about gender, sexuality, or any other part of who you are—is always at risk of being disseminated to friends and family, but also to people you do not know. At times, identity disclosure can help young people experience a greater sense of authenticity in their relationships and provide them access to social support from various network members, leading to a greater sense of well-being, according to the *International Journal of Environmental Research and Public Health* study about disclosure, particularly on Facebook. They may also find more opportunities to be civically engaged. On the other hand, if disclosure happens inadvertently or in an unsupportive context, that can lead to "the loss of support and experiences of rejection or victimization," with negative impact on a young person's psychological well-being.

Sometimes disclosure can happen in ways you wouldn't think of—such as someone adding you to an LGBTQ group or offhandedly including you in a reference to LGBTQ individuals. There is little you can do to control such incidents besides clearly articulating to your loved ones and acquaintances who know about your gender identity or sexual orientation how you are presenting yourself publicly on social media. And likewise, be conscientious of how your own online behavior could potentially reveal someone else's identity without their consent.

Discuss your intentions to disclose with supportive friends and family.

DON'T FACE IT ALONE

As you decide when and where you want to disclose your sexual orientation or gender identity further, think about first doing research, and don't be afraid to talk to peers or adults who already have gone through a similar experience. Discuss your intentions with supportive friends or family members so they can be prepared to give you support and encouragement along the way. Especially having a supportive adult on your side can give you confidence in case a truly negative situation arises at school, work, or other social environments.

TEXT-DEPENDENT QUESTIONS

1. Who is the best person to go to if you are experiencing challenges or harassment at school or work?

2. What are indications that your school or workplace fosters an environment that is accepting and supportive of LGBTQ individuals?

3. How much more likely are LGBTQ youth to be harassed or bullied online or via text message than non-LGBTQ youth?

RESEARCH PROJECTS

1. Research the laws governing workplace discrimination in your state. What employment-related rights do you have as an LGBTQ person, and what can you do if you experience discrimination at work?

2. Post something innocuous on a social media site, such as Facebook or Instagram with a note saying that you are seeking to have the information shared. Watch to see how quickly that information gets passed to not only online acquaintances, but to people you do not know as well.

5

Finding Community, Large and Small

BINARY SYSTEM: *Something constructed by people in a group or society to try to organize complex things into only two parts, such as male/female or girl/boy.*

INTERNALIZING: *Unconsciously or consciously accepting or absorbing an idea, opinion, or belief so it becomes part of your own mindset or character.*

LIVING OPENLY: *The phase after actively coming out, when a person has intentionally or selectively shared their gender identity or sexual orientation with loved ones, and now fluidly tells the new people who come into their life when and how they choose.*

STIGMATIZING: *The act of unfairly disapproving of, condemning, or negatively labeling a person or a behavior as wrong or shameful.*

As most LGBTQ individuals will confirm, coming out is an ongoing process that extends throughout a person's life, especially in a society filled with straight and cisgender assumptions. For example, same-sex couples may frequently face the assumption that they require two bedrooms instead of one when staying at a hotel or looking for an apartment.

Many people may find that the process becomes easier as they mature and grow more comfortable with who they are. Rather than actively coming out, they may eventually find themselves simply **living openly**. Others may always feel that their sexual orientation or gender identity is a very private part of their life and remain selective about whom they share it with for a variety of reasons.

External factors—such as family dynamics, the culture and political climate within one's community, or an LGBTQ-unfriendly workplace—may influence how comfortable a person is with sharing their identity at different times of their life.

Hopefully, people will see your identity as part of what makes you unique.

PRACTICING PATIENCE

It is normal to have expectations about how people will respond to you coming out, as well as to hope that their reactions will be positive. The hope is that people will be very accepting and see your gender identity or sexual orientation as just one more part of what makes you wonderfully unique.

In some cases, though, people will need time to adjust when this new information is shared by a teenager identifying as LGBTQ. For a variety of reasons—none of which has anything to do with

People might experience a number of emotional responses when you come out.

Work to establish an ongoing dialogue with the person you come out to.

you personally—they might experience a number of emotional responses when you come out to them. For example, they might feel honored, disbelieving, relieved, angry, anxious, curious, surprised, uncomfortable, or simply unsure of what to do next or how to support you. The best thing to do is to be patient and not react strongly in turn. Remember that you also might have needed time to make discoveries and come to terms with your own gender identity and/or sexual orientation.

Especially if you share a meaningful relationship with the person, give them time to process and adjust, answer their questions, and work to establish an ongoing dialogue. That will provide both parties the opportunity to foster understanding, which is key to creating sustainable relationships.

That doesn't mean that a teenager identifying as lesbian should not reference her girlfriend when talking to a peer just because it could make them uncomfortable at first, or that a transgender student should

"I really wanted her to know my partner and that I had found healthy love."

not ask to be identified by their preferred gender pronouns. Being patient simply means not **internalizing** negative or apathetic reactions and being gracious, while allowing the other person to change their mind or come around to being a supportive ally.

"I WANTED TO SHARE"

At 20, Elizabeth decided to come out formally to her mother because she wanted her to meet the same-sex partner she "was very much in love with."

"I really wanted her to know my partner and that I had found healthy love," says Elizabeth, who identifies as pansexual but also does not subscribe to ideas of **binary systems**. "Being so happy with a woman, I wanted to share that happiness with her."

Because of their close mother–daughter relationship, Elizabeth also thought her mom might suspect she was not straight. At first, Elizabeth's mother responded that while it is alright to struggle with

It feels like a betrayal to hear someone describe you as bad or wrong.

such feelings, they are meant to be packaged up, neglected, and repressed. That was upsetting for Elizabeth, but it also revealed to her that her mother might also have dealt with bisexual feelings and been conditioned not to explore them. As for Elizabeth, who at a very young age started becoming aware she was attracted to humans regardless of sex or gender, feels grateful that she didn't want to "shove those feelings in a box." She expressed that to her mother and was told in response, "This is the one thing you're not supposed to be."

"There are so many awful actions we can take as human; to hear that this was the worst really struck me to the core," Elizabeth says. It also felt like a betrayal of sorts to hear someone to whom she had given so much of her love and energy to describe her identity as "bad or wrong."

I HAVE ALWAYS BEEN ME

Rather than lashing out at her mother or allowing the bitterness to swell, Elizabeth was able to recognize her mother was coming from a place of fear and misunderstanding. She sensed, Elizabeth explains, "that I was here to love in a way that was scary to her."

"She knew I would get my heart broken, and my feelings would take me into sexual terrain that she was raised to code as perverse," she says.

Elizabeth confronted her mother gently but frankly. Elizabeth reminded her mother that while she was growing up, her mother would frequently recognize and compliment the person she was, "whose love is so freely flowing and wants to move toward all people." She recalls telling her mother, "You knew I had the capacity to be attracted to any person. That's always been who I am."

Elizabeth's mother softened after being challenged in that way. Though it took years of conversation and patience as she dismantled her prejudices, the two were able to heal their relationship as a mother and daughter. Something Elizabeth was also able to recognize is that her mother had been socialized to mischaracterize non-heterosexual life as a sort of sex addiction. She had also been raised to **stigmatize** women taking pleasure in sex, in general.

Recognize that others may be coming from a place of fear and misunderstanding.

Elizabeth's mother was able to realize when her daughter was truly happy.

Over time, Elizabeth remembers, "It really took her seeing me with my same-sex partner, making dinner, or dancing a slow dance, and seeing it be tender and soft and loving and not sexual or oozing with desire."

When Elizabeth and her partner amicably decided to end their relationship, her mother "tried to use her social charm to woo us back together," Elizabeth says. That signaled a level of healing insomuch as Elizabeth's mother was able to realize when her daughter was truly happy and wanted her to continue being happy.

"She was able to find peace with it," says Elizabeth, who is now 29. Her mother passed away in 2014, after a struggle with a degenerative memory disorder.

SURROUNDED BY A TRIBE

Throughout their lifetime, all individuals who identify as LGBTQ are almost certain to encounter someone who is simply not accepting or kind about their identity. When rejection happens, do not be

All LGBTQ individuals are certain to encounter someone who is not accepting or kind.

You can seek connections on a national level through online communications.

discouraged. You are not alone, and there are literally millions of people globally who identify as LGBTQ, and even more who consider themselves allies. Find these people, and build connections to them. As PFLAG notes, they will understand what you are going through, whether they have been there in the past or are currently coming out themselves.

BeLonG to Youth Services, a national organization supporting LGBTQ individuals in Ireland, interviews young people about coming out to their peers as part of its Stand Up! LGBTQ Youth Awareness project.

GETTING INVOLVED IN A GROUP

Getting involved in an organization specifically designed for LGBTQ youth is a great place to start. As mentioned in the previous chapter, an increasing number of schools have GSA clubs that connect youth, not only to other LGBTQ students and allies at their school, but also to peers and mentors from across the world. These clubs are also overseen by a teacher or faculty adviser, which puts the young people in touch with at least one supportive, trustworthy adult.

Many communities, especially in larger metropolitan areas, also contain local chapters of national organizations, such as PFLAG. These groups offer young people a variety of resources and support services. People in rural areas may be more challenged to find local LGBTQ youth organizations and social clubs. That doesn't mean they are alone or need to feel isolated. If a young person cannot find a group in their hometown, they can seek connections on a statewide or national level through online communities. The Trevor Project and Gay, Lesbian, and Straight Education Network (GLSEN) are two very helpful organizations.

Many communities include LGBTQ community centers.

Q CENTERS AND OTHER SAFE SPACES

Many communities include LGBTQ community centers—sometimes called Q centers or other names, depending on the city or region. Many of these local centers provide not only camaraderie and representation, but also tangible resources, such as mentorship, social events, meal sharing, referrals for health care or mental health care, and a safe space to hang out or decompress. College campuses also often have a center that provides support services to LGBTQ students and allies. Knowing the location and contact information of a local LGBTQ center in your community can be useful in case a situation arises when you need support in some way or another. You can search for LGBTQ centers in your city, county, or state via lgbtcenters.org.

Several organizations provide helplines.

AT A LOSS

Some young people may still feel truly alone, finding no one they can trust or are yet comfortable talking with. Several organizations provide helplines, where a teenager can connect with a supportive and understanding person without giving their name. Anonymous support lines, such as the GLBT National Youth Talkline (800-246-7743) or the Trevor Project's 24-hour lifeline (866-488-7386) are good resources to turn to if you feel at a loss for where or how to begin building a network of support. You also may be able to e-mail questions confidentially to help@ LGBThotline.org or live chat with a friendly and knowledge support person online at www. GLADAnswers.org. These are just a few resources available to you, and there are plenty more to assist you in times of need.

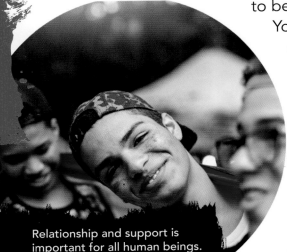

Relationship and support is important for all human beings.

A LITTLE HELP GOES A LONG WAY

Seeking help or support is hardly a sign of weakness. Every person needs camaraderie, encouragement, and advice from time to time, and they access this through a variety of relationships to parents, siblings, friends, mentors, educators, and others.

Relationship and support are important for all human beings but can be especially crucial for LGBTQ youth as they become aware of their gender identity or sexual orientation, learn about accepting themselves, and then discover ways to disclose this identity to other people in their lives.

No one is expected to go it alone, and through the increasing availability of clubs, online communities, organizations, and hotlines, you will not have to.

TEXT-DEPENDENT QUESTIONS

1. What is the distinction between actively coming out and living openly?

2. How can you be prepared to handle negative reactions, and in what sorts of positive ways can you respond?

RESEARCH PROJECTS

1. Research your local community, and try to find a social group, organization, or agency that could provide support services if you ever need them. Copy down the address and contact information to keep on hand.

2. Research various organizations to see what sorts of support services, such as helplines, they provide. Keep a copy of this information. Even if you do not need it, someone else you encounter might.

SERIES GLOSSARY OF KEY TERMS

Agender (or neutrois, gender neutral, or genderless): Referring to someone who has little or no personal connection with gender.

Ally: Someone who supports equal civil rights, gender equality, and LGBTQ social movements; advocates on behalf of others; and challenges fear and discrimination in all its forms.

Asexual: An adjective used to describe people who do not experience sexual attraction. A person can also be aromantic, meaning they do not experience romantic attraction.

Asexual, or ace: Referring to someone who experiences little or no sexual attraction, or who experiences attraction but doesn't feel the need to act it out sexually. Many people who are asexual still identify with a specific sexual orientation.

Bigender: Referring to someone who identifies with both male and female genders, or even a third gender.

Binary: The belief that such things as gender identity have only two distinct, opposite, and disconnected forms. For example, the belief that only male and female genders exist. As a rejection of this belief, many people embrace a non-binary gender identity. (See **Gender nonconforming.**)

Biphobia: Fear of bisexuals, often based on stereotypes, including inaccurate associations with infidelity, promiscuity, and transmission of sexually transmitted infections.

Bisexual, or bi: Someone who is attracted to those of their same gender as well as to those of a different gender (for example, a woman who is attracted to both women and men). Some people use the word bisexual as an umbrella term to describe individuals that are attracted to more than one gender. In this way, the term is closely related to pansexual, or omnisexual, meaning someone who is attracted to people of any gender identity.

Butch, or masc: Someone whose gender expression is masculine. *Butch* is sometimes used as a derogatory term for lesbians, but it can also be claimed as an affirmative identity label.

Cisgender, or cis: A person whose gender identity matches the gender they were assigned at birth.

Coming out: The process through which a person accepts their sexual orientation and/or gender identity as part of their overall identity. For many, this involves sharing that identity with others, which makes it more of a lifetime process rather than just a one-time experience.

Cross-dresser: While anyone may wear clothes associated with a different sex, the term is typically used to refer to men who occasionally wear clothes, makeup, and accessories that are culturally associated with women. Those men typically identify as heterosexual. This activity is a form of gender expression and not done for entertainment purposes. Cross-dressers do not wish to permanently change their sex or live full-time as women.

Drag: The act of presenting as a different gender, usually for the purpose of entertainment (i.e., drag kings and queens). Many people who do drag do not wish to present as a different gender all of the time.

Gay: Someone who is attracted to those of their same gender. This is often used as an umbrella term but is used more specifically to describe men who are attracted to men.

Gender affirmation surgery: Medical procedures that some individuals elect to undergo to change their physical appearance to resemble more closely the way they view their gender identity.

Gender expression: The external manifestations of gender, expressed through such things as names, pronouns, clothing, haircuts, behavior, voice, and body characteristics.

Gender identity: One's internal, deeply held sense of gender. Some people identify completely with the gender they were assigned at birth (usually male or female), while others may identify with only a part of that gender or not at all. Some people identify with another gender entirely. Unlike gender expression, gender identity is not visible to others.

Gender nonconforming: Referring to someone whose gender identity and/or gender expression does not conform to the cultural or social expectations of gender, particularly in relation to male or female. This can be an umbrella term for many identities, including, but not limited to:

> **Genderfluid:** Someone whose gender identity and/or expression varies over time.

> **Genderqueer (or third gender):** Someone whose gender identity and/or expression falls between or outside of male and female.

Heterosexual: An adjective used to describe people whose enduring physical, romantic, and/ or emotional attraction is to people of the opposite sex. Also **straight**.

Homophobia: Fear of people who are attracted to the same sex. *Intolerance*, *bias*, or *prejudice* are usually more accurate descriptions of antipathy toward LGBTQ people.

Intergender: Referring to someone whose identity is between genders and/or a combination of gender identities and expressions.

Intersectionality: The idea that multiple identities intersect to create a whole that is different from its distinct parts. To understand someone, it is important to acknowledge that each of their identities is important and inextricably linked with all of the others. These can include identities related to gender, race, socioeconomic status, ethnicity, nationality, sexual orientation, religion, age, mental and/or physical ability, and more.

Intersex: Referring to someone who, due to a variety of factors, has reproductive or sexual anatomy that does not seem to fit the typical definitions for the female or male sex. Some people who are intersex may identify with the gender assigned to them at birth, while many others do not.

Lesbian: A woman who is attracted to other women. Some lesbians prefer to identify as gay women.

LGBTQ: Acronym for lesbian, gay, bisexual, transgender, and queer or questioning.

Non-binary and/or genderqueer: Terms used by some people who experience their gender identity and/or gender expression as falling outside the categories of man and woman. They may define their gender as falling somewhere in between man and woman, or they may define it as wholly different from these terms.

Out: Referring to a person who self-identifies as LGBTQ in their personal, public, and/or professional lives.

Pangender: Referring to a person whose identity comprises all or many gender identities and expressions.

Pride: The celebration of LGBTQ identities and the global LGBTQ community's resistance against discrimination and violence. Pride events are celebrated in many countries around the world, usually during the month of June to commemorate the Stonewall Riots that began in New York City in June 1969, a pivotal moment in the modern LGBTQ movement.

Queer: An adjective used by some people, particularly younger people, whose sexual orientation is not exclusively heterosexual (e.g., queer person, queer woman). Typically, for those who identify as queer, the terms *lesbian*, *gay*, and *bisexual* are perceived to be too limiting and/or fraught with cultural connotations that they feel don't apply to them. Some people may use *queer*, or more commonly *genderqueer*, to describe their gender identity and/or gender expression (see **non-binary** and/or **genderqueer**). Once considered a pejorative term, *queer* has been reclaimed by some LGBT people to describe themselves; however, it is not a universally accepted term, even within the LGBT community. When Q is seen at the end of LGBT, it may mean *queer* or *questioning*.

Questioning: A time in many people's lives when they question or experiment with their gender expression, gender identity, and/or sexual orientation. This experience is unique to everyone; for some, it can last a lifetime or be repeated many times over the course of a lifetime.

Sex: At birth, infants are commonly assigned a sex. This is usually based on the appearance of their external anatomy and is often confused with gender. However, a person's sex is actually a combination of bodily characteristics including chromosomes, hormones, internal and external reproductive organs, and secondary sex characteristics. As a result, there are many more sexes than just the binary male and female, just as there are many more genders than just male and female.

Sex reassignment surgery: See **Gender affirmation surgery**.

Sexual orientation: A person's enduring physical, romantic, and/or emotional attraction to another person. Gender identity and sexual orientation are not the same. Transgender people may be straight, lesbian, gay, bisexual, or queer. For example, a person who transitions from male to female and is attracted solely to men would typically identify as a straight woman.

Straight, or heterosexual: A word to describe women who are attracted to men and men who are attracted to women. This is not exclusive to those who are cisgender. For example, transgender men may identify as straight because they are attracted to women.

They/Them/Their: One of many sets of gender-neutral singular pronouns in English that can be used as an alternative to he/him/his or she/her/hers. Usage of this particular set is becoming increasingly prevalent, particularly within the LGBTQ community.

Transgender: An umbrella term for people whose gender identity and/or gender expression differs from what is typically associated with the sex they were assigned at birth. People under the transgender umbrella may describe themselves using one or more of a wide variety of terms—including transgender. A transgender identity is not dependent upon physical appearance or medical procedures.

Transgender man: People who were assigned female at birth but identify and live as a man may use this term to describe themselves. They may shorten it to *trans man*. Some may also use *FTM*, an abbreviation for *female-to-male*. Some may prefer to simply be called *men*, without any modifier. It is best to ask which term a person prefers.

Transgender woman: People who were assigned male at birth but identify and live as a woman may use this term to describe themselves. They may shorten it to *trans woman*. Some may also use *MTF*, an abbreviation for *male-to-female*. Some may prefer to simply be called *female*, without any modifier.

Transition: Altering one's birth sex is not a one-step procedure; it is a complex process that occurs over a long period of time. Transition can include some or all of the following personal, medical, and legal steps: telling one's family, friends, and co-workers; using a different name and new pronouns; dressing differently; changing one's name and/or sex on legal documents; hormone therapy; and possibly (though not always) one or more types of surgery. The exact steps involved in transition vary from person to person.

Transsexual: Someone who has undergone, or wishes to undergo, gender affirmation surgery. This is an older term that originated in the medical and psychological communities. Although many transgender people do not identify as transsexual, some still prefer the term.

Further Reading & Internet Resources

BOOKS

Albertalli, Becky. *Simon vs. the Homo Sapiens Agenda*. New York: Balzer & Bray, 2016.

Written by a former clinical psychologist, this young adult coming-of-age novel explores coming out in a way that is both moving and cliché-free.

Gray, Lee-Anne, PsyD. *LGBTQ+ Youth: A Guided Workbook to Support Sexual Orientation and Gender Identity*. Eau Claire, WI: PESI, 2018.

A comprehensive and practical workbook full of worksheets, handouts, and practices that help adolescents and their caregivers better understand sexual identity, gender norms, and fluidity and deal with the challenges of coming out.

Madrone, Kelly Huegel. *GLBTQ*: The Survival Guide for Queer & Questioning Teens*. Minneapolis: Free Spirit Publishing, 2003.

Featuring practical advice, real-life experiences, and accessible resources, this encouraging and frank book explores the challenges faced by LGBTQ teenagers, such as prejudice, discrimination, and rejection.

Marcus, Eric. *What If?: Answers to Questions About What It Means to Be Gay and Lesbian*. New York: Simon & Schuster, 2013.

A helpful guide that provides answers to more than 100 questions for those who are curious about their own sexual orientation or looking to support someone close to them who identifies as LGBTQ.

WEB SITES

GLAAD. www.glaad.org
A dynamic media force established in 1985, GLAAD is devoted to national advocacy and education that advances human rights for LGBTQ individuals. GLAAD works through news, digital media, and entertainment to promote a narrative for the LGBTQ community that accelerates acceptance.

GLSEN. www.glsen.org
Founded in 1990, GLSEN (pronounced "glisten") is a U.S.-based education organization dedicated to creating safe and inclusive K–12 schools for all students, regardless of sexual orientation and gender expression/identity.

GSA Network. www.gsanetwork.org
The GSA Network is a coalition that trains youth leaders and supports LGBTQ youth organizers across the country to take action and create change at all levels through GSA clubs. The network's mission is to unite trans and queer youth for racial and gender justice.

Human Rights Campaign. www.hrc.org
America's largest national LGBTQ organization, the Human Rights Campaign represents more than 3 million members and supporters nationwide as it works toward ensuring basic equal rights for LGBTQ individuals at home, at work, and in the community.

It Gets Better Project. www.itgetsbetter.org
The mission of the It Gets Better Project, an international nonprofit organization, is to uplift, empower, and connect LGBTQ youth around the globe. This movement, established in 2010 as a social media campaign, provides hope and encouragement to young LGBTQ people, reinforcing the message that "it gets better."

The Trevor Project. www.thetrevorproject.org
Founded in 1998, The Trevor Project is a leading national organization that provides life-affirming services to LGBTQ youth younger than 25. The organization's programs and services include crisis interventions, suicide-prevention trainings and resources, and community resources, including online communities.

PFLAG. www.pflag.org
The PFLAG motto is, "Because together, we're stronger." The organization is the extended family of the LGBTQ community, comprising LGBTQ individuals, family members, and allies. With approximately 400 chapters and 200,000 nationwide (including the District of Columbia and Puerto Rico), the organization advances equality through support, education, and advocacy.

INDEX

Author's Biography

Katherine Lacaze is a freelance writer and children's theater director who resides in the illustrious Pacific Northwest. Since graduating with a degree in journalism in 2011, she has written articles and stories for a wide variety of newspapers, magazines, Web sites, blogs, and other publications across the United States. Along with her affinity for writing, she possesses a passion for education, working with young people, and advocating for the rights and well-being of the LGBTQ community.

Credits

COVER

(clockwise from top left) Dreamstime/Santiago Nunez Iniguez; Dreamstime/Lentolo; Dreamstime/Beavera; Dreamstime/Rawpixelimages

INTERIOR

1, Dreamstime/Wavebreakmedia Ltd; 3, Dreamstime/Rawpixelimages; 11, Shutterstock/lev radin; 12, Dreamstime/Diego Vito Cervo; 14, iStock/Kirkez; 15, Dreamstime/Beavera; 16, Dreamstime/Lentolo; 17, Dreamstime/Stokkete; 18, iStock/digitalskillet; 19, Dreamstime/Hans Slegers; 20, Dreamstime/Lei Xu; 22, Dreamstime/Brainsil; 23, Dreamstime/Epicstock; 24, iStock/Sladic; 25, Dreamstime/Alberto Jorrin Rodriguez; 26, Dreamstime/Viacheslav Iacobchuk; 28, Dreamstime/Wong Chee Yen; 30, Dreamstime/Paul Simcock; 31, Shutterstock/1170490822; 32, iStock/Graphixel; 33, Shutterstock/John Arehart; 35, iStock/Roberto Galan; 36, Shutterstock/Morgan DDL; 37, Shutterstock/Santypan; 38, Shutterstock/Aamir M Khan; 39, iStock/Kall9; 40, iStock/Rawpixel; 41, iStock/tommaso79; 42, iStockGustavoFrazao; 44, iStock/monkeybusinessimages; 46, iStock/KatarzynaBialasiewicz; 47, iStock/Kall9; 49, Shutterstock/Shutterstock.com; 50, Shutterstock/Worldstock; 51, iStock/CasarsaGuru; 52, iStock/Martin-DM; 53 (UP), iStock/Vladimir Vladimirov; 53 (LO), iStock/Juanmonino; 54, iStock/GustavoFrazao; 55 (UP), iStock/pixdeluxe; 55 (LO), Shutterstock/35037523; 56, Dreamstime/Wrangler; 58, iStock/SolStock; 60, Shutterstock/Frantic00; 61, iStock/skynesher; 62, iStock/filadendron; 64, ClarkandCompany; 65, iStock/Steve Debenport; 66, Dreamstime/James Kirkikis; 67, iStock/TwilightShow; 68, iStock/LeoPatrizi; 69, iStock/CourtneyK; 70, iStock/Bernardbodo; 72, iStock/Mlenny; 74, iStock/LeoPatrizi; 76, iStock/petrych; 77, iStock/Bongojava; 78, iStock/Suriya Silsaksom; 79, iStock/FatCamera; 80, iStock/ti-ja; 82, Shutterstock/Kamira; 83, Shutterstock/Shutterstock.com; 84, Shutterstock/Shutterstock.com; 85, Shutterstock/Shutterstock.com; 86, iStock/FG Trade; 87, iStock/Ma Felipe; 88, iStock/FG Trade